I0159211

IF I COULD TELL HER

HEAR HIM OUT OR WEAR HIM OUT

ANTHONY MORALES

GEM
bookclub

DEDICATION

FOR JAYDEN

Jayden
Your Journey Continues...

Blessed are the pure in heart, for they shall see God.
Blessed are the peacemakers, for they shall be called the children of God.
—Matthew 5:8-9

Jayden's Journey...
Our Journey Continues Through You...Thank You

TO THE READER

"YOU ARE THE MASTER OF YOUR TIME & THOUGHTS. WITH TIME AND THOUGHT, POSSIBILITIES ARE LIMITLESS." - THE THOUGHT MASTER

From Anthony Morales, The Thought Master

To create our best lives, we must have clarity as we embark on our journey to create more love, success, and happiness. I would like you to start this book with clarity regarding the title, *The Thought Master*. Specialists are surrounding us. Experts who can, and will, reveal to us how to deal with our funds, our well-being, our youngsters, our garden, our golf – even our sexual experiences and our burial service game plans.

Clinicians and employment questioners will hand us identity evaluation tests and disclose to us where we fit into the scheme of human instinct or vocation inclinations. From time to time are we urged to comprehend who the absolute master is? You are the best teacher in your life. You have inside of you all the solutions to your particular inquiries concerning yourself.

You have the inward intelligence as of now to realize what you have to do and how to do it. What squares us is the feeling that we don't have the foggiest idea, or the inward voices that rehash the old messages that we heard as kids (more often than not about not being adequate or unworthy).

When we start to hear our strong, genuine voice, we can access that internal intelligence. At the point when individuals come to see me and I reveal to them that I can offer them no counsel, they are at times shocked; they begin to perceive that looking for exhortation from someone else whom they assign as "the master" is a piece of the old, educated example of surrendering their particular power.

As a Life Enrichment Speaker and Motivator, the purpose of my life is to help you refrain your thoughts and bring balance to the mind, body, and spirit and hand back the mark of a master to where it has a place. I am the master of my thoughts. I am The Thought Master. You are the master of your thoughts. You are The Thought Master and together we are The Thought Masters. We are the Thought Masters of our collective consciousness of minds, bodies, and spirits. We are many Thought Masters under one humanity. With time and thought, possibilities are limitless.

PEACE & Love, Anthony

YOU OWE IT TO YOURSELF TO FEEL YOUR BEST!

IMPORTANT! PLEASE READ.

*N*ever substitute professional therapy for self-help **books, books and resources!**

* * *

Although, Anthony Morales does **not recommend any self-help book as a substitute for professional therapy**, *If I Could Tell her* and *The Thought Master Life Enrichment* series and coaching programs should prove immensely illuminating to anyone who would like to create more success in their professional and personal life.

THE THOUGHT MASTER
ENRICHMENT & COACHING
PROGRAMS

*W*ould you like to be able to communicate with more clarity and bring about more balance to your mind, body and spirit? Would you like to be able to enrich your life and find more love and success?

ANTHONY MORALES' new self-help book, *If I Could Tell Her*, takes you on a journey of exploration, both to the past and to your present, to reveal the path to happiness and success in both your private and work life. It doesn't matter what your relationship status is, what sexuality you are, how much you earn, your stage of life or when you started, this book will provide the tools for success with chapters that include:

THOUGHT MASTER'S secrets to communicating love with quality time
    Affirmative words
    Physical touch
    The roots of rejection

And much more...

BY READING it you can improve relationships, including the one you share with God, through a narrative of personal essays. Anthony Morales applied the principles of vulnerability to transform the way he lived, loved, healed, partnered and parented, and now you can do the same by learning it through his breakthrough program, **THE THOUGHT MASTER.** Get a copy of **If I Could Tell Her** today and see what it will do for your life.

Would you like to be able to communicate with more clarity and bring about more balance to your mind, body and spirit?

VISIT ANTHONY ONLINE AND SCHEDULE A FREE INTRODUCTORY COACHING SESSION TODAY.

THE THOUGHT MASTER ENTERPRISES

WWW.THETHOUGHTMASTER.COM

*A*nthony Morales, inspirational speaker, and life enrichment coach is the author of "If I Could Tell Her" and the creator of **THE THOUGHT MASTER** life enrichment coaching programs.

VISIT *WWW.THETHOUGHTMASTER.COM* FOR MORE MOTIVATIONAL & Inspirational Books & Guides to Goal Setting and Achieving your Dreams in Life and Business by **Anthony Morales** (Life Enrichment Series).

THE THOUGHT MASTER ENTERPRISES
    Copyright © 2018 by Anthony Morales, Thought Master
    All rights reserved.

NO PART of this book may be reproduced in any form or by any electronic or mechanical means, including information storage and retrieval systems, without written permission from the author, except for the use of brief quotations in a book review.

TITLE: IF I COULD TELL HER
   Subtitle: *Hear Him Out OR Wear Him Out*
   Edition: 2nd Edition
   By: ANTHONY MORALES
   Genre: Self-Help
   Category: Love & Relationships
   ISBN-13: 978-1-59825-099-2

IF YOU FIND ANY ERRORS, typos, reference omissions, mistakes or you would like to have your contribution including in an upcoming release, contact us online via a contact form on website www.globalexecutivemedia.com or email info@globalexecutivemedi-a.com 1-708-4-ebooks (708) 432-6657.

Publisher: Contact the Cheryl Katherine Wash www.cherylwash.com with questions, errors or concerns with this edition.

To contact the author, Anthony Morales, visit www.thethoughtmaster.com and fill out and submit to via the contact form.

GEM BOOK CLUB

IMPRINT OF GLOBAL EXECUTIVE MEDIA

Chicago, Illinois

WWW.GEMBOOKCLUB.COM
WWW.GLOBALEXECUTIVEMEDIA.COM

SPEAKING REQUESTS & BOOK SIGNINGS

Request Anthony to be a speaker at your next event, book club meeting, book signing, literary event, seminar, workshop, and community event.

CONTACT

Phone: 1-84-Thought-1 (1-848-468-4481)
Email: anthony@thethoughtmaster.com

Download the EPK (Electronic Press Kit:
https://www.thethoughtmaster.com/media

STAY CONNECTED

www.facebook.com/thethoughtmaster |
www.twitter.com/thoughtmastera
www.Instagram.com/thethoughtmaste

GIFT A COPY TO YOUR PARTNER &
FRIENDS

EBOOKS, PAPERBACKS AND HARDCOVERS
CAN BE ORDERED ONLINE OR ANYWHERE
BOOKS ARE SOLD.

Title: IF I COULD TELL HER
Subtitle: Hear Him Out OR Wear Him Out
By: ANTHONY MORALES
Genre: Self-Help
Category: Love & Relationships
Price: $24.99 (+Shipping)
ISBN-13: 978-1547265978

PRAISE FOR ANTHONY MORALES

IF I COULD TELL HER

* * *

"Anthony is an amazing speaker! You can hear truth in his words through the passion of his delivery. He's caring, understanding, and his incredible book 'If I could tell her' takes you on a journey that could help you to resolve issues in your relationships, and help you to achieve your life goals."

—Koby Dumas
Launch Pad Radio, Your PersonalGPS

"Sharp, Brilliant, High Motivation! Who wouldn't want to walk away with those qualities after hearing Anthony."
—Gerald Bell
DeVos Urban Leadership

"Anthony Morales, The Thought Master, has given the world a powerful new way to look within."
—Cheryl Katherine Wash,
Author of My Private Room, I opened the door and there was light…,

ACKNOWLEDGMENTS

* * *

I am grateful to my *Omaida*, for her assistance and patience and encouragement on the many long evenings and weekends that were spent in preparation of this book and events and this includes the help from all of you in my biological and extended family, friends, colleagues and countless community partners. Special thanks to the reader. You are the lighthouse! I would also like to thank the families of the people like you that allow you to support me and the men and women who participated in focus groups, surveys, events, interviews, volunteers, sponsors, humanitarians, *The Thought Master History Makers* and *The Thought Master Mind Team*.

PREFACE

* * *

Anthony Morales is passionately self-assessing, reflecting, research-ing, and evolving while writing self-help books and coaching programs. *IF I COULD TELL HER*, and the subtitle is 'HEAR HIM OUT OR WEAR HIM OUT' is his latest project. Join us in our LIVE events, *"Conversations with Anthony"* so you can help empower other couples which will help individuals, families, men, women and chil-dren in creating more success in their lives. The book's foundation is based on his personal life story, experience, and research. I invite you to be open because he is coming from a different place that is not mainstream. We strive to create our best lives by speaking from our hearts with the hopes of healing and rebuilding ourselves and others.

PROLOGUE

"We want to be that man in your life, who can love you the way you desire and deserve, but most of us are not familiar with that kind of love, or what it means because we've never had it and were hoping to get it from you and not from someone else; yet, we don't know how to tell you. We want to share with you when we're afraid, weak, can't meet your expectations and that we need you just as much as you need us. But we don't know how because all we've been taught is that a real man must find the way out or find the answer even if it kills him and sadly that's exactly what's happening every day to men by the thousands. There were times when we took the risk and told you the truth about how we felt about something and your response shocked us and hurt so bad that we promised ourselves not to trust you or any other female again with our feelings."

—**Anthony Morales, Author of *If I Could Tell Her: Hear Him Out Or Wear Him Out'***

THE THOUGHT MASTER

"With time and thought, possibilities are limitless."

-Anthony Morales, The Thought Master

FOREWORD

As a woman, I encourage women to take the time to read this book and then share with your partner. We invite you to give us feedback and join #tellher campaign on social media www.ificouldtellher.com and www.thethoughtmaster.com.

I believe that women have the power to help men understand that it is okay to be vulnerable in order to heal and rebuild. But we all must look within. This book can be read by women and men. This book is for anyone who is looking to better communicate with their significant other.

Let's start with the women and share this book with your partner. Gift this book to a girlfriend and people you know who are struggling in their personal and professional lives. I encourage you to collaborate and join our success network. There is a need to help women understand the men in their lives.

As we are aware, social norms in many cultures have associated the act of men sharing *how they feel and being open as a sign of weakness and vulnerability.* Anthony wants to bring more women to a higher level of consciousness regarding the challenges that men have in expressing their emotions, feelings, desires, and thoughts. The goal of the book is to help men and women enhance their communications with their partner by looking within and self-assessing how you communicate with your soul mate.

I want to end by saying, I support Anthony for many reasons. He was there for me and was able to coach and motivate me through an unimaginable event. *The untimely death of my child,* ***Jayden****.*

Anthony was there for me when my special needs son, ***Jayden****,* made his transition to the next phase of his spiritual journey. ***Jayden's Journey*** continues. Anthony's personal life experiences from a time-honored previous marriage and his current journey have prepared him for this next journey.

Anthony has vowed to donate proceeds from his books and events to creating a ***foundation*** to support women with resources and programs to help them create more success in their lives and the lives of their children with special needs and disabilities

Happy Reading!

*I hope you enjoy **If I Could Tell Her** by Anthony Morales*
and inbox us your testimonials and reviews.
Omaida Acevedo
Co-Founder, The Thought Master Enterprises
Founder, Jayden's Journey Foundation
Owner, Farmers Insurance Agency Franchise - Garfield, New Jersey

INTRODUCTION

> "SELF-DISCOVERY IS SELF-CONSCIOUSNESS WITH A HEIGHTENED SELF-AWARENESS THAT STARTS WITH SELF-REFLECTION LEADING TO INNER AND OUTER TRANSFORMATION. YOU HAVE TO KNOW WHERE YOU COME FROM TO KNOW WHERE YOU ARE GOING."
> —ANTHONY MORALES

After 33 years of marriage and thousands of hours of man talk, I believe it is time to help women (wife, girlfriend, partner) understand that men have much to say to them about how we feel. There are many reasons (for lack of a better word) why we are not saying what we want and are crying down deep inside to share it with someone special.

Discovering the ways to express ourselves is one of the most complicated and frustrating things that we experience daily, and I believe most men will die this way; literally. I'm sure culture and upbringing play a role in how we express ourselves; nevertheless, we must do all that we can to overcome this anaconda constraint that is destroying our lives and loved ones.

Ladies would you like to discover what are some of the pitfalls in communicating with your man? Do you believe that there's more to the relationship than what you're experiencing? I've personally come to a point in my life that I decided to start telling the woman close to me how I think and feel about our relationship because tomorrow is not promised to any of us. This does not give me or any other man the right or permission to dishonor, disrespect or hurt them, but it does give us the opportunity to express ourselves. Men are you ready to give HER your best by sharing what's on your heart? And are you ready to experience a love like never before? For the record, I want to let the brothers out there know that the men that I'm referring to are not incapable of standing on their own two feet; they can and will accomplish so much more.

And for my sisters, these are good men who are trying their best with what has been handed to them and with what they've had to learn just to survive. If someone would just STOP and LISTEN, maybe he could have an opportunity to create more healthy, loving and prosperous relationships. God knows we need it.

My desire is to help women understand and to learn more about male figures in their lives. I would like to offer men guidance by sharing my personal story, experiences, and data collected during my countless conversations with women and men to help them in their relationships. I have also invited other men from different walks of life to express what each wish they could tell the woman in their life, why they can't or won't share with them how they feel, and what recommendations do they suggest to the female population in helping us be more expressive.

Yes, ladies, we might not be as sensitive and expressive as you are by nature, but there are times that you'll say or do things that wound us so deeply and hurts so bad that it drives us to isolate ourselves, or hurt others because we don't know how to handle the matter or we're too proud to ask for help.

We want to be that man in your life, who can love you the way you desire and deserve, but most of us are not familiar with that kind of love, or what it means because we've never had it and were hoping to get it from you, not from someone else; yet, we don't know how to tell you. We want to share with you when we're afraid, weak, can't meet your expectations and that we need you just as much as you need us.

But we don't know how because all we've been taught is that a real man must find the way out or find the answer, even if it kills him; and sadly, that's exactly what's happening every day to men by the thousands.

There were times when we took the risk and told you the truth of how we felt about something and your response shocked us and hurt so bad that we promised ourselves not to trust you or any other female again with our feelings.

My passion is to help men by showing them that they are not alone in this journey of isolation, due to a lack of awareness of how to share our hearts with the woman we love. I am confident that the female in our lives desires to hear us share our hearts with them because in my experience it has helped heal, build, strengthen, add security, love and value to the relationship. I believe that if men become more expressive with their partner, and they are received with love and understanding, there will be less tragedy in our families and society.

Men, it's possible for us to share our hearts especially with the woman who has stood by our side through thick and thin, while everybody else who we expected to stay with us walked out. Was it easy for me? Hell no! High risk, you better believe it. Was it worth it? Yes, with every ounce of blood in me. This all started because one day I asked myself, *If I Could Only Tell Her,"* how I feel, what would my life be like? This is not to say that your outcome will be like mine. This is the reason why I'm writing this book so that you'll have some reference guide to use and apply and hopefully get the results you and your loved one desires.

I believe that you are one of those serious women and men who have made the decision and commitment to take on the **'If I Can Tell Her'** journey that will last a lifetime with great rewards and challenges each step of the way. Is it going to be easy? No. Is it possible? Yes.

I had the pleasure and honor to interview women and men who allowed me to hear their heart in regard to this matter. You will be enlightened with what they had to say. All of the contributions and conversations were amazing, and I wish I could include them all in the book, but you find some great feedback toward the back of book where you will meet with men who've been in many relationships and some who have remained committed for years and men from different walks of life. You'll discover that every one of them were able to relate to this internal epidemic that is destroying men and families.

I believe without a doubt that the men and women who read this book will be able to relate to the information and connect with one of these stories and hopefully find the story insightful where your level of awareness will be enlightened, and you'll find a breakthrough for a happier life and relationship.

As I said earlier, this book is intended to help women and men who desire to improve their relationships with each other. I trust that you will join me on this journey and help me help as many people as possible especially the younger generation. Throughout the book, I will recommend how to prepare yourself for the moment of expression, the timing and atmosphere, and how to maintain progress throughout the journey. I will also include other resources to help you along the way. Come and join me on this journey and together we will discover the precious diamond in your relationship.

1

IGNORANCE YOUR ENEMY

"TO KILL YOUR GOOSE THAT LAID THE
GOLDEN EGGS IS IGNORANCE. TO BE
IGNORANT OF ONE'S STUPIDITY IS NOT
AN EXCUSE— AND IT IS CLEARLY NOT
BLISS. " —ANTHONY MORALES

*G*rowing up a child in a single parent home with five siblings was an adventure within itself. It was a "blessed-mess." What is a *blessed-mess*? A *'blessed-mess'* is the ability to understand something challenging or overwhelming immediately, without the need for conscious reasoning. I intuitively allowed my intuition to guide me through chaos until I began the self-reflection process to begin the self-discovery journey.

Let's start with Mom! My mother was so overwhelmed that at times she would find herself frustrated with the responsibilities of keeping things in order while living in poverty. We survived from instinct rather than conscious reasoning and now with clarity, I can talk about it today. This was a challenge for us as kids, especially for me because my two older siblings had the same dad; the three younger ones had a different dad; and I had a different father from everyone else.

Finding myself in this position as the only child of my father's made me feel like the **black sheep of the family**—literally! (*I had the* *darkest complexion)* in the family and was reminded of this on a regular basis by my siblings which caused me to isolate myself from them. As a child I was not aware that colorism *(dark vs light skin)* and skin-bleaching was a world-wide epidemic then that still plagues more than people of afro-descent like the Japanese and Europeans today. *(I personally never bleached then or now)*. Therefore, I had no idea had to deal with the teasing. It felt more like rejection. This carried into my youth which didn't help my skinny little body when it came to confront those who took advantage of me, like my classmates, co-workers, employers, even family members. *(I personally never bleached then or now)*.

I felt helpless and useless because I was afraid to speak my peace of mind *(if they could see me now)*. I remember as a young man trying to fit in with others my age and how I felt inadequate because of my inability to express myself the way that I wanted and wished to.I never knew how to deal with this isolation and no one helped me, which really sucks because a lot of *BS* that I experienced could have been avoided *(that felt good to say)*. Unfortunately, this isolation crept into my marriage and hung around for a very long time and caused some serious damage to my self-esteem and my family.

When my ex-wife *(I will refer to **her** as **HER** to protect **HER** identity and to respect **HER** because I know now it was not **HER** it was due **to** (**me**) **HIM** having to look within and so forth)* **and I took time to talk, SHE did most of the talking and made most of the decisions many years into the marriage.** While I agreed with HER, when shit hit the fan I was always looked at as an incapable husband and father which made me feel humiliated in public.

I remember our teenage daughter while riding in the car with us heard a conversation between her mother and me of an incident that she was aware of. When she noticed my passive response, she called **ME** a, "**PUNK**" because I was intimidated by her mother. This frustrated me and caused me to isolate myself even more because of embarrassment and shame which undoubtedly affected my image as a man.

I was immature and ignorant of what was happening and a little too proud to admit that I had a big problem which I didn't know how to handle. I remember HER asking me what's wrong with you when she saw me quiet and calm. I would always tell her those famous words; "nothing—I'm ok," because to express myself was a major challenge and a battle. Come to think of it, I was a **disaster**. **Thank God** that I made it this far.

As time went by, I knew this had to be fixed or else my home was going to crumble, and many innocent people were going down with me. But I was not about to let that happen on my watch. I made up my mind that I was going to take the bull by the horns and take charge of this way of thinking that was holding me back and destroying my family.

I knew that I had to confront myself in this area of isolation and the fear that if I spoke up things would get out of order. I had to find a way to make it happen without hurting anyone or making things worse because in the past I've caused a lot of pain and loneliness.

So, I decided to speak more of my mind when it came to family matters and how I felt about certain things. Mind you, this was not common practice for me to do because HER ran the house and I just went along. You can imagine what that must have looked like in front of the kids and public. Just the thought of speaking up made me nervous and afraid; not because of her, but because of myself. The concern of being shut down, misunderstood or the whole situation backfiring at me would cause me to get frustrated and angry which would create chaos.

Now for the record, HER was and still is an amazing woman, mother and grandmother; but in the beginning, she was a total control freak and very dominant which she picked up from her mom (*I should have caught onto it in the beginning. I blame it on love.*) and undressed it in our marriage. Needless to say, that I was a very passive, insecure, weak-minded man who had no idea what the hell I was getting myself into, all because I wanted to be loved. **Sounds familiar anyone?**

Ok, back to my taking the bull by the horns. I remember one day while we were on vacation in West Virginia with the boys, we decided to let them stay up in their room while HER and I got ready to re-explore each other.

While getting ready, one of the boys came out of his room to get something to eat that his mom told him not to. This got her very upset. I decided to step in and save the moment. Before I knew it, **Mr. Hyde** (*Dr. Jekyll and Mr. Hyde's split personality problems*) * showed up and I could not figure out what to do while the boys looked on in shock.

I kept my cool as I usually tried to for the sake of peace and the well-being of the relationship, which I realized later on was the wrong thing to do. Maybe if I would've confronted her, today we would still be together, or we would have separated a long time ago.

Let me also mention that after being married a few years, I realized that I had married my mother, not my wife. So, I had to divorce my mother and marry my wife. Let me explain. I was always in search of some motherly love from my mom as a child, but because of all the chaos in our house and my mom as a single parent, love wasn't always equally divided.

There also were times, because of my immaturity and irresponsibility as head of house that I put myself in a humiliated position which reminded me that as the man of the house I had to take charge. That, of course, was totally foreign to me because I had no idea what that meant due to the fact that I came from a completely dysfunctional single parent home. Talk about being frustrated and almost going insane. Really! There were times I thought about submitting myself into a mental institution, and I even experienced a time of depression for about six months; even worst, I thought about suicide.

Now I can't put it all on her because I was going through some other stuff, and I was no little angle. In fact, I had very low self-esteem and issues with my family's distance from me and other things which I didn't know how to deal with that affected my relationship with HER. I remember having anger outbreaks which would cause her to fear me and stay away.

There were times when we were driving down the road and would get into an argument; and because I didn't know how to handle the argument, I would drive faster to the point that I would bring her to tears. Or when we were in our bedroom talking about keeping ourselves healthy and in shape, and she responded in a way that got me angry; and I started punching the wall till I made a big hole in it. Come to think of it, I was pretty cruel.

As time went by, a paradigm shift starting to happen in my response to her which showed that I had built confidence in myself, courage, and maturity to confront her on many issues that were troubling me. I don't know if it was an act of God or some revelation that I received from Him; but whatever it was, it was working.

Eventually, I took a step and shared with her how I felt about certain things in our relationship. I knew it was going to be risky and I must admit I was afraid of what the outcome might be because of previous experiences which caused me to isolate myself, or completely shut down, or turn to other things; nevertheless, it had to be done if we were to grow stronger and live longer together.

I asked her to be open to what I was going to share and not hold it against me because that would only draw me further from her. I started telling her that I was not happy in our sexual relationship, spiritual differences, physical (her body), our economic status and that I knew that there was more for both of us, but we had to get past this point.

My form of expression was honest, sincere, sensitive and real. At times, I became a little upset because she was not being receptive to what I was saying and feeling. I just wanted to call it quits and let the internal death in me continue and lose all hope of peace. But I knew down deep inside that this would be wrong; why? Because I've quit for many years and not much had changed which made me feel like I was dying and insecure of our future together.

As I continued all seemed well, then the conversation started taking a different course because fault finding came into play and I could tell by her body language that she was not up for what I was sharing. This made me uncomfortable, and I knew that I had to cut it short for the sake of another opportunity.

That night I went to bed before her, and she remained in the living room. Before I knew it, she was crying which made me sad because my intention was not to hurt her but to share my heart. Did I make a mistake? Was it the wrong timing? Is it really worth the frustration? So many questions went through my mind. "Should I just live with this bleeding heart of hurt for the sake of not bringing pain to the one I love? But what about me and how I feel?" As I was falling asleep, she came to bed crying softly so not to disturb me. I didn't know what to say or do; yet, I knew I had to make a move of love. This is my wife I said to myself.

Finally, I moved over and held her close to me. There were no words; the closeness said it all. The next day while driving, she told me that I hurt her the night before when I spoke. I told her that it was not my intention and I tried to be as sensitive as possible. All I wanted to do was share my heart. Then I asked the question, how? She then told me that it was not so much of what I said, but how I said it. I then apologized and promised to be more sensitive and careful of how I would share my feelings.

Because I was willing to admit that I was wrong, this opened a major door to discover something that was lying down deep inside of my wife for many years before we met and during our marriage that was slowly eating her away that I was not aware of. As I sat and listened, I saw my wife break down like a little girl reaching out to me for help and protection. I was lost for words and felt helpless, but I knew that this was my time to put into practice what I've gained through my time with God.

After she had shared with me what had happened, I was upset with myself for not paying attention to the most important person in my life. I was unconsciously contributing to her childhood pain and slowly killing the one that deserved my best. As the days went by, the conversation continued. She spoke and I listened with my heart, mind, ears and eyes, then something amazing started happening; the more receptive we became to each other, the more love and peace we received.

My words were few, but selective; and as I was sharing my heart, I felt a bonding happening like never before, one that I've longed for all of my life. Throughout this whole process, we were both being healed and together becoming one as God had intended. Later in one of our discussions, we admitted that we were not happy with each other and that we had two completely different lifestyles.

Sadly, to say, things did not turn out for the best in the relationship. A mutual agreement was made that a separation would be best for both of us. Sounds crazy, right? I still can't make much sense of this ending. It's been about five years since the writing of this book that we separated and divorced. I fail not to mention that much recourse were utilized including three years of marriage counseling; but at the end, it was up to us.

My ignorance and stupidity, which I take full responsibility for, was part of the outcome of my former marriage. Nevertheless, I'm at peace within and I've learned a valuable lesson, which is to love myself and to walk in the freedom of wise expression while helping improve the quality of life for others.

I share this information with you because I like to keep things clear and real, as you will see throughout this book from the other men and me. Hopefully, you will not be discouraged but will continue to read on and learn some very important lessons about life and relationships.

The moral of my story is that ignorance and the lack of taking charge (speaking up) on a matter that is affecting the relationship is not bliss and must be addressed right away. Seek all the professional help that you can get to try to save the relationship with that special man or woman in your life before it's too late.

A word to the guys: I know that expressing ourselves is not common practice for us thanks to the media, society, past experiences and other influences. Nevertheless, this is no excuse for us to live in an isolated emotional state of being that is eating at us daily and taking away from who we are. I remember telling, HER, my former wife, that if she would only take the time to control her "**HER-motions**', 'SHE-**motions**', and stopped listening to "**HER-self** talk to **HER-self**," that she would discover a man that she never knew she had by her side, who after 33 years of marriage all I wanted to love her and spend my life with **HER**. Unfortunately, we (HER & HIM) killed the goose that laid our golden eggs—*communications*. We didn't understand that "communication" is the key to anything golden that our heart's desires in life.

Guys, you have to give your HER or your future HER more than a fair chance before you finally give-up and move on to find a new HER and or the next chapter in your life. If you keep doing the same thing with each HER you meet, you will get the same results. The breakdown in communications by blaming and finger pointing without self-reflection will continue to kill your goose that produce your golden eggs.

To the gals: we guys are not as emotional as you are. Therefore, we might not express ourselves the way you might see fit and convincing. Nevertheless, we do hurt when you say or do things to us. But in most cases, we suppress our feeling and words to avoid looking weak and stupid because of the pain that we are experiencing which might cause us to respond in a way that will create chaos.

When you ask us to tell you what's on our mind, be prepared because we might tell you in a way that we see fit for us based on where we are at in life at that moment; and if you really want the raw truth, then put your emotions to the side and don't take it so damn personal.

You might also consider letting us talk till we can't anymore. Let us cry, get upset or even walk away till we're ready to continue. Also hold yourself back from interrupting us just because you want to make a point clear or justify a case. Because if you don't, you might frustrate us and never hear us talk to you from our heart again.

I recommend that you both seek guidance to understand how to set some guidelines when speaking to avoid a disaster like no yelling at each other, no hurting each other emotionally or physically, no fault finding. I think you get the point; and always remember if it gets too hot, respectfully excuse yourself and walk away to avoid a disaster or saying something you cannot take back.

STRANGE CASE OF DR. JEKYLL AND MR. HYDE is a gothic novella by the Scottish author Robert Louis Stevenson first published in 1886. The work is also known as The Strange Case of Dr. Jekyll and Mr. Hyde, Dr. Jekyll and Mr. Hyde, or simply Jekyll & Hyde.

2

A HAPPY MAN. A HAPPY LIFE

"HE CANNOT MAKE HER HAPPY AND SHE
CANNOT MAKE HIM HAPPY. WANT THE
BEST FOR EACH OTHER. WANT THE BEST
FOR YOURSELF. GIVE YOURSELF
PERMISSION TO MAKE YOUR HAPPINESS
A PRIORITY." —ANTHONY MORALES

There's an old saying that says, "**A happy wife is a happy life**" which has some validity to it, but it also has caused many changes in families and relationships. I know of many men who do just that; they put a lot of effort into keeping the relationship with their wife by keeping her happy at the expense of expressing his emotions. I experienced this in many cases dealing with men when I counseled them as I served in the past as the Senior Pastor at our church, and I must say it was sad.

These were men who loved and took good care of their family, who understood the importance of their role as a husband and a father and were even willing to die for their loved ones. But actually, they were not happy, not because they were family men, but because they were not free to express their emotions on how they really felt about themselves, their relationship or any other thing that was important to them.

They would go through the spiritual rituals with the hope that somehow in a divine way God would intervene and fix the problem. I must say that very few of them, to my recollection, ever saw a major breakthrough. I was always baffled with how the wives of these men would take them for granted and later on wonder, why is he being so cold? I had to contain myself and be wise and selective with my words as I tried to help them make sense of their ignorance and stupidity. Women want men in their lives who will love, protect and provide for them and their children as he should, but there are some women who won't accept him telling her the truth about how he really feels about a particular matter.

For example, if you ask him how to do I look in this dress? In his mind he is trying his best to tell you without hurting you that you look a little fat in it, it's ugly or any other thing that has gotten you or any other female upset in the past, which caused him some backlash and hurt that he experienced for being honest. He might tell you exactly what you want to hear and even put his integrity on the altar and sacrifice it just to keep the peace in the relationship. He will do this because he loves you to the point of denying and being truthful himself.

Because of previous experiences, he's going to lie to you just to keep the peace in the relationship and to make sure you don't deprive him of a piece for the next few weeks. After a while, his performance will get so good (which might qualify him for a Tony award) that it will become a normal practice in the relationship; and although you might pick up his lack of honesty, you will accept it or even disregard his opinion which is a sign that the relationship is ill or becoming ill. There is a point where he will disconnect emotionally from you not because he wants to, but because in order for him to function in the relationship as the man that you expect him to be, he will suppress himself and just go with the (your) flow.

In many cases when a man disconnects himself emotionally from his woman, he does it to protect himself from any pain that relates to past issues. For example, I would always avoid any conversations with HER that dealt with living a healthy lifestyle because it would turn into a mess. I was into exercising and eating healthy and she didn't really see the importance of preparing ourselves for our future together when we grew old. She would take it as an insult against the way she looked when I brought up the issue. Therefore, I would refrain from expressing my thoughts regarding a healthy lifestyle, which in turn made me sad because all I wanted was to help prepare for an active future.

So being happy for me became an illusion, a fantasy, a strong desire to be open with her that slowly died with me and we both lost out on an opportunity to discover the riches within each other. This type of scenario causes men to look for happiness in other things like hanging out with the boys, spending more time at the office or the gym or to pick up a habit of drinking or some other thing which will create a bigger gap in the relationship.

I believe that most men who have a strong desire and an interest in staying in a relationship have a true, sincere heart, and they would do anything to keep the peace. But here's the catch, you'll never get to know the true man who you say you love which means you're living with a stranger who you trust with your life and that is a reality that most women are living with and most likely don't know it.

That, my dear, sucks and if you think that was rough, you ain't seen nothing yet. Now just to soften things out a little, we have to take a few steps back and find out if your man is at peace with himself because if he's not, that might be a good place to start. This is going to take some work from you and him and might also require some professional help to have a major breakthrough.

A man needs to find peace within himself which most men that I've dealt with don't know how. Many turn to religion and get results which are not always a guarantee, while others turn to someone or something hoping to find that inner peace. As a partner, you can only enhance what he already has in his heart and no more.

So, don't kill yourself trying to make him happy when he must do that for himself. Now I'm no expert peace finder, but what has worked for me was when I started to take time out to love myself, to give myself the best things that gave me a sense of inner peace. I forgave myself for all the things that I did to others and to the most important person in the world, me. I started taking better care of my body by eating better, exercising and becoming more aware of my thoughts by what I listened to, read and watched.

I also became very selective with the people who I invested my most precious commodity which is my (life) time. This meant close friends and family members who refused to take responsibility and action for their life and expected someone else to do it for them. I learned to accept and value myself and not let other outside forces dictate my life and future.

The first part of every morning is dedicated to me, not to the news, work, family or whatever else, but to me. This has allowed me to see myself differently and get to know the man that I am and to discover that I am unique and special which has helped me to see myself in a way that I've never seen in the past. The more time I committed to myself, the more I became aware of what needed special attention in me that no one else can do for me but me.

This brought on a level of peace, love, focus, confidence and inner strength which has affected my life in a powerful positive way; started new relationships, grown my business, and now I'm helping others improve their quality of life as I've always dreamed of. This all started when I decided to make time for me and commit myself to that decision.

This allows me to give the best of the best to others and never run out. As a woman, you have the power to help bring healing to the relationship. When you see him happy, join in and add as much to the moment as possible.

Do you remember those moments when you've seen him so happy that it makes you smile? That is the best time for you to draw closer to him, because that is when he is vulnerable and open to share his heart with you. This is a perfect moment in the relationship where you want to be open with what he wants to express to you; this will help you see beyond what you normally experience. The scriptures tell us that a happy heart is like medicine to the bones.

"Forgiveness is not an occasional act: It is an attitude."
    ~ **Martin Luther King, Jr.**

3

"WHEN HE STARTS TO FLOW, LET HIM GO!"

"STAGNANT WATER ATTRACTS BACTERIA AND STANDING WATER CAN CAUSE PERMANENT STRUCTURAL DAMAGE TO YOUR STRUCTURE. A MAN MUST FLOW LIKE HEALTHY RIVERS BECAUSE HIS IS THE LIFELINES AND WATERSHEDS OF OUR PLANET." -ANTHONY MORALES

*I*t's been said that most men talk less than women; you and I know that's a fact. They've even come up with scientific research to prove it, and it's all because of the *Foxp2** protein. (**Forkhead box protein P2 (FOXP2)** *is a* protein *that, in humans, is encoded by the FOXP2* gene, *also known as CAGH44, SPCH1 or TNRC10, and is required for proper development of speech and language.*)

I Wonder What The Protein Has To Say About That.

It has previously been claimed that women speak about 20,000 words a day — some 13,000 more than the average man. That's more words than in this entire book. I think that it's a beautiful thing that a woman can be so expressive with her thoughts, emotion, and feelings. I'm sure some of you men can remember when you were a boy while playing you fell and got a *boo-boo* and you ran to mom because you knew that just her words were enough to bring healing to the wound, and you knew that after the words, came the touch that took away the pain and you were back on your way again.

Funny that most boys don't run to their dad, but that's a whole different discussion. It's also been proven that most men can shut down and not be freely expressive with their emotions, thoughts and feelings unless they're having sex, are angry, watching sports, drunk or hanging out with the boys.

But with all that, I believe that most men are constipated emotionally and you ladies can play a very important role as a powerful emotional fiber source. If fact, you are so powerful that you can actually customize — not make — your man, bet that got your attention; will talk about that later. As a child, men have been trained to limit expressing our emotions in public because of the ridicule and shame that comes afterwards and not to mention dad's pride being hurt.

But there are times when a man starts to flow in expressing his emotions; it could be because of death in the family, loss of his job or something that's very important happened to him which is affecting his emotions.

Now when he gets to that point, ***Let Him Go!*** As long as he can in sharing his feelings (unless he is being abusive to you) you will learn so much about the way he thinks, what's going on inside of him, his perspective of life and how he handles crisis. At this moment, you need to be very patience and wise and not allow your perception of life to be the only tool used in guiding him through this time of his life. I know that he might not be making any sense or keeps repeating the same thing over and over again to the point that it's boring or annoys you; but if you want to help him, you must be patience.

As a woman, you have learned to be more sensitive to your intuition which has helped you throughout your life. I'm sure you can relate that when you've talked to him in the past, all you wanted was for him to listen and show that he cares by being loving and patient. Another thing that you must be aware of is to turn off the conversation in your head with yourself that has made a mess in the past which turned him off and stopped him dead in his tracks and has affected the relationship.

One thing that used to cause me to stop talking in my previous relationship was when I started sharing something important, I would be interrupted because she could not wait till I was finished to say something. I would then stop sharing my heart and let her talk, and it would go on for a while before she became aware that I was not in the same frame of mind. When you see that he's in the flow, you got to let him go! This will give you enough information to help him set up a plan and get some positive results. That's how powerful you are.

WARNING! If you're ever tempted to use any of the information that he shared with you when he made himself vulnerable against him for whatever reason, make sure it's because you plan to completely end the relationship and never get together again. Because it will surely somehow come back and bite you in the butt.

This is why you have to keep your emotions in check when he's sharing his heart with you if you want to avoid him going deeper into an ibis of emotional shutdown. Let me just interject something here for the ladies, if you're looking for a man to be emotionally open with you, I suggest that you do your homework before you get involved; it will save you a lot of heart pain. Here are some things to look for: Does he communicate with the females in his life? Does he respect and honor them? Is he open with his emotions? Does he become angry easily?

THESE ARE some of the things that will give you some insight on how he will relate to you and the success of the relationship. There's power in how you keep him in the flow of sharing his heart with you, but you must be wise; and the greatest motivator must be love, first for yourself then for him. Here are some powerful actions that you can take in keeping your man in the flow and believe me you will enjoy the results.

But before I tell you, let me make you aware they must become a way of life personally for you before you can pass it on; otherwise, it will turn out to be a disaster. First, there must be respect in the relationship for each other; but if you've ever taken notice, the females in the majority of the cases are the ones who respect the most and with that being the case, you have the upper hand.

This upper hand is very powerful and must be used with love and wisdom so that you can get the results that you know are possible for the success of the relationship. For example, when he gets upset and angry at you and starts yelling and you respond and not react to him by asking him if he loves you and if he does why does he speak to you that way.

Or you walk away and when things clam down, you share with him that you're concerned for his well-being. This might sound corny, but it's better than going toe-to-toe with him and adding more fuel to the fire.

HAVE you ever been in a relationship with a guy who you learned how to guide to the point that the results were so astonishing that people were taking notice, starting with his family? The respect that you render to him is not so much because he deserves it, but because you respect yourself; so, when you give it, it comes out so powerful that it helped him to stay in the flow and to trust you to help him build a healthy and strong relationship with you and others.

You might say yeah! But if he doesn't respect me, why should I respect him? Simply because he doesn't know how to respect himself and this is where you have to ask yourself the question, do I love him enough to guide him through this process? If so, then take full charge with love and wisdom; and if not, get the hell out and move on to better things or someone else. Life is too precious, and love is too valuable.

Second, you have to be patient because most (immature) guys come into a relationship with a warped perception of what love is and some never come out of that mentally. If you were to ask a guy what love is, you might find yourself stupefied by the response, not because he knows, but because he thinks he does and he might be very far off from what you're ready for.

But let's just say you're already in the relationship and you really love this guy, and you know that things can work out because although he's totally oblivious to what love is, he still knows how to love you. You decide that you want to become more serious with him and you're ready to take on the challenge.

This is where patience, self-restraint from killing him or yourself, love and wisdom come into play. Because assuming that he knows or should know might not be the best way to deal with him, and when you put him in that place of knowing just because he's a man, is an irresponsible thing for you to do. First of all, he might not admit that he doesn't know which is a normal sign of ego, pride, ignorance or just plain stupidity.

Whatever the case is, remember that you are in a powerful position in guiding him through; but you have to let him flow and go so that you can get enough information to help him make sense of what he's saying. Because if you let your ego, pride, ignorance and stupidity get in the way, you will cut the flow and he may never allow himself to go there again.

Third, love on him again even if you feel he doesn't deserve it. I remember a few years ago, I became unfaithful to a beautiful lady who truly loved me as I've never experienced before and I took her and her love granted. I felt disgusted, like a low-life and I was beating myself up to the point that it was affecting my life.

Then she did the thing that I least deserved and expected, she loved on me. That's right! She saw in me what I didn't see in myself, a man who lost himself in a way of thinking that caused pain to all involved in the affair. The love that she gave me by putting her ego and pride aside set me free and showed me the true power of a woman. This action that she took has allowed me to learn to love and respect women.

Most of all, I came to realize that my perception of life was not reflecting my true value of myself as a man. Today, I am free to "Flow and Go" with my emotions.

4

WOMAN, YOU CAN CUSTOMIZE
YOUR MAN

"A STRONG WOMAN BUILDS HER WORLD. SHE IS WISE ENOUGH TO KNOW THAT IT WILL ATTRACT THE MAN SHE WILL GLADLY SHARE IT WITH." —ELLEN J. BARRIER

The closest person in a boy's life is his mother from the womb, throughout childhood and in many cases throughout manhood. This bond is like an external umbilical cord that feeds him emotionally as he grows throughout life and when it's cut off too soon, for whatever reasons, the results can be devastating.

This is how powerful the role a woman plays in the life of a man. That's why when you're seeking the perfect man **(whatever that means)** you must not get so caught up on just his looks or how he entertains you, but you MUST go deeper. As I said earlier, find out how he loves and cares for the closets females in his life. This will help you determine if he's a good candidate for you to invest your life in a relationship with him and it will also help you stay focused on what you really want from a man who would love and care for you.

If you don't take the time to go deep into his perception of life and how he sees women, then you might end up deeply wounded and hurt for a very long time.

So how do you customize (not make) your man? It all starts with you. In order to customize your man, you have to be at a point in your life where you love yourself fully, and it shows completely in your lifestyle. This will put you in a position where you can impart in him certain values, characteristics, and habits that will enhance him as a man and help strengthen the relationship. Now remember, your intentions and motives must be driven by a true love that is not for self-gain or because you don't want to lose your knight in shining armor to someone else.

Oh, by the way, he must be just as intentional as you are and do his part in this process as well, or else you might end up creating a monster.

I WAS CUSTOMIZED

Let me explain. As a child, I was a loner due to the fact that I was the only one who had a different father from my siblings. As I mentioned earlier, this caused me to be closed with my emotions because I was not given the opportunity to share my feelings or when I did, the support that I received was not encouraging me to continue to make the effort.

But when I found that special lady who saw in me those qualities of a man that were powerful; and unknowing to me, she started helping me see myself as I could be, and not as I was. She patiently and wisely started customizing me with wisdom, love and respect. When she saw me stepping out of my character (as the loving and powerful man she saw), she would lovingly remind me that my reaction was not conducive to the man that she saw in me.

Now I must admit that I found this approach strange and manipulative because it was foreign to me and I didn't understand it. There were times when I had to make a very important decision that could have affected my future and I would discuss it with her and she would in a wise way highlight something that I had overlooked; but here's the catch, she never made me feel like I was incapable of making the decision, or when I watched her as she dealt with strangers and the love that she showed them which caused me to reevaluate how I dealt with people, or how she never made me feel like less of a man when I couldn't figure certain things out that might have been simple to her but complicated for me.

Even if I were breaking and down, and many people turned me away, she still saw me as a good man who was worthy of her love. Little did I know that she was customizing me to be the kind of man that she wanted to have a relationship with and I fell in love with her. Interesting that there were times that she did certain things to me or for me that made me wonder if she had this all planned out because it seemed so well orchestrated and smooth.

Then one day I asked her if she had this all planned out? And her answer was yes before you came into my life. Ladies don't underestimate yourselves or sell yourself short just because you feel that time is running out and you find yourself desperate which causes you to settle for less than you deserve.

There are good men out there who are on the lookout for a woman like you. Eventually, you will find each other and when it happens, you'll both know; and the main indicator will come from the core of your being because it will have little to do with the external. It's been just over a year that we've been together, and I must say that I truly love her and I'm madly in love with her.

I am now free to express my emotions like never before; I cry more, laugh more, share more of what's in my mind and heart, act like a nerdy little boy; and I am at peace with myself and many people have taken notice. Today, I have lived over a half century and I know with thought and time, possibilities are limitless and look forward to the next journey.

I can truly say that I'm happy and look forward to growing more into this new man who I can say I love. I know how to "LOVE ME!" and I will continue to grow and evolve my mind, body and spirit. As I've learned from my personal experience, it all starts with how we see ourselves which helps us in how we can customize our lives and future.

5

GENTLEMEN, REHEARSAL IS OVER; IT'S TIME TO LIVE OUT YOUR ROLE

"WE MUST MOVE ON FROM REHEARSAL TO REALITY IF WE REALLY WANT TO ENJOY LIFE, AND MAKE A CHANGE FOR THE GOOD." —ANTHONY MORALES

I was acting up in school and had to be sent away to an educational facility somewhere in the countryside of New Jersey for special kids like me. As I entered my teenage years, things got more complicated where drugs and gangs became part of my life. I was on a down spiral before I even got a chance to enter manhood. Yes, there were men who took time with me who gave me guidance, but that lasted for a short time which left me hungry for more. What's even sadder was that none of those men were family members; they were all strangers with a loving heart. God bless all of them for their contribution to my manhood. This hunger for love led me to HER, my former wife who at the age of around fifteen, I met in a youth group at a local church. Her undivided attention led me to seek her out and make her my girlfriend who I was hoping would make up for the lack of love that I was seeking at home.

Yet, after several years into the marriage, I became more passive and would rather keep the peace than deal with the confrontations. I'm sure a lot of men can relate. That's why I said earlier that a happy man, a happy life (if you're not happy with yourself, you'll make others sad), because in society men are still expected to be the head of the household; but when it comes to his emotions, in many cases they get swept under the carpet.

I remember as a child living at home with my mom and five siblings, and our dads were nowhere to be found. As a child, it would devastate me when I would see a little boy doing special things like fishing, bike riding and other things that a little boy enjoys doing with his father. I couldn't understand why my dad wasn't around to share those beautiful moments with me, which made me sad, confused and sometimes angry to the point where I was acting up in school and had to be sent away to an educational facility somewhere in the countryside of New Jersey for special kids like me.

As I entered my teenage years, things got more complicated where drugs and gangs became part of my life. I was on a down spiral before I even got a chance to enter manhood. Yes, there were men who took time with me who gave me guidance, but that lasted for a short time which left me hungry for more. What's even sadder was that none of those men were family members; they were all strangers with a loving heart.

God bless all of them for their contribution to my manhood. This hunger for love led me to HER, my former wife who at the age of around fifteen, I met in a youth group at a local church. Her undivided attention led me to seek her out and make her my girlfriend who I was hoping would make up for the lack of love was seeking at home.

At the age of eighteen, we got married (I had no idea what on earth I was doing) and I was on my way to a life I always dreamed of — someone to love, care for me and be there for me whenever I needed her (can you pick up the selfish immaturity?).This dream went on for about two years, then came a baby girl and a few years later, the boys.

Rehearsal was over, it was time to live out the role of manhood, husbandhood and fatherhood. Have you ever seen a chicken running around with its head cut off? That was me at its worst. The first thing that I wanted to do was to run home to my mama and hide behind her for protection because I was being consumed with responsibilities that were totally foreign to me.

But I remember the promise that I made to myself, which was that I was not going to abandon my family the way my father did to me. It was time to live out the role, forgetting the past and doing my best for the future of my family. But how? I had no idea, no role models and I was too proud to admit that I was completely clueless about handling my crisis. The only place I knew was the local church (not the same one where I met HER because they were too righteous).

There I was able to observe other fathers who were more experienced than I and I watched them closely which allowed me to mimic what they were doing with their children which worked in many cases for me. This along with reading the Bible, books from Dr. James Dobson, Tony Evans and others helped me raise a family that today I am very proud of.

There were times when I wanted to give up, and walk out like a lot of fathers did and still do today, but all I thought about was the promise that I made to myself when I was a young boy of not doing what my father did to me. Today my daughter is a domestic engineer (stay-at-home mom) with two beautiful daughters and my two sons are professional barbers with a growing barber shop business. My awakening came in my late thirties from rehearsal to living out my role.

I stayed in rehearsal far too long; while focusing on manhood and fatherhood and living those roles out on a daily basis, I remained in rehearsal in the area of husbandhood. Let me explain. My dedication to our children was intense because of the lack of having a father in my life. I immersed myself in giving them the best that I was able to give them. I attended basketball games, track meeting, school plays, PTA meetings, karate classes, went bike riding, fishing and camping. I did it all.

I was determined to be their best role model as a father so that they could have what I never had and give them what they would need when they became parents. On the other hand, I was stuck in rehearsal when it came to being a husband and for some reason or another, I couldn't get out. When it came to living out the role as a husband, I found myself falling short and going back into rehearsal. I think I know why this happened. I believe that keeping the peace (rehearsal) in the relationship was easier than confronting HER on issues that were troubling me, and that made me feel uncomfortable.

Yet, after several years into the marriage, I became more passive and would rather keep the peace than deal with the confrontations. I'm sure a lot of men can relate. That's why I said earlier that a happy man, a happy life (if you're not happy with yourself, you'll make others sad) because in society men are still expected to be the head; but when it comes to his emotions, in many cases they get swept under the carpet. Now, to set the record straight, I take full responsibility for not dealing with the issues that were overwhelming me and not seeking out the right professional help to help me go from rehearsal to living out the role as a husband. I'm sharing this because I realized that I let things go too far and didn't address the issues when I should have. I didn't put as much effort into the relationship as a husband as I did as a father and maybe, just maybe, I would still be married if I had.

The lesson learned throughout this journey is that I didn't take the time to deal with issues that I was dealing with within myself. I was so fixated on what was happening outside of me instead of inside. I was insensitive to my feelings and my emotions because I thought that they didn't matter as much as other people and things did. I desensitized myself to protect my heart from being hurt over and over again which just added to what I was still dealing with from childhood, and to avoid responding in an ill-manner that would have caused me to lose my family.

My state of mind at that moment did not allow me to see beyond myself; therefore, I couldn't reach HER where she was — and that caused us to drift away slowly as the years went by. I wasn't able to Read Her so that I could Lead Her; to see her not with just my eyes, but to shut down all of the self-talk that my ego was telling me; to put my pride aside and to find a way to compromise, even if it meant losing just to win her back closer to me, and to each other; to listen with all of my being and not with my perception of what I thought it should be .

This experience has allowed me to grow into the man that I am today and to take time out for myself daily and give myself the very best possible. To forgive myself and others who have hurt me, and to ask for forgiveness for hurting them.

Men we have to find every possible way to communicate with our woman — one we say we love; and women, you have to try all that you can by taking time to listen to what your man has to say so that you can reach the man that's in your life, which you say you love — if you believe that he is the man that you are willing to live your life with.

6

GUYS IT'S TIME TO SET THE STAGE

"THE SEXIEST THING THAT A MAN CAN DO TO A WOMAN IS TO CRAWL INSIDE OF HER MIND AND MAKE HER IMAGINATION RUN WILD". —ANONYMOUS

*T*he beauty is in setting the stage with the best props you can create. Imagine adding every color, aroma, feeling, touch and ambience that you can draw out from within yourself that is part of her and use them as props. This stage has to be prepared so well that you become one with it, to the point that you're so fully engaged that you mesmerize her; where she can see your love, sincerity, and concern for her and the relationship.

This must be done with the right motive and not because you're trying to manipulate or hurt her. It has to come from that place in your heart that you protect from others who would try to hurt you. You have to crawl inside of her mind and make her imagination run wild, but before you can do that you have to be there already.

I know that this is deep for some men, but stay with me. It's nothing new. Then you can open up to her slowly and carefully as you start sharing your heart as freely as you can. She will be receptive because she'll take notice of your effort to introduce her to a moment that is as special as she is. I know that this might sound like hard work for some guys, but you should be used to it. I mean isn't that the way you got her in the first place?

Just keeping it real, gentlemen. Remember, we're no longer in rehearsal; it's time to live out the role. This takes time and practice; but if you really love her, you'll prepare yourself as long as you have to with the best that you can find. Getting intimate with her sexually doesn't need to be a part of it, just get sexy using your imagination.

Sir, if this doesn't work, you might want to consider taking her to a psychologist and possibly leaving her behind, or maybe to a morgue, or just resuscitate her with your love. Men we have to be willing to go as far and as deep as we need to. Also, we need to be wise and loving as we have been created to be to help her become more aware of who we really are.

Life is too short and it was never created to last forever on this earth, so we have to give her the very best or move on with our lives. Take it from a man with 33 years of experience in a previous marriage where I learned a lot of powerful life-changing lessons from the love and pain, the good and bad that I was part of which I'm sharing with you.

You've come this far in life by the grace of God or whoever you want to give credit to, and you're probably with a woman you truly love. So, the choice is yours to live on with her or to move on by yourself. If she's still with you, there's a good chance that she has hope that you will come through and reveal yourself to her and move beyond where you are to where you both desire to be in the relationship. Before I make any recommendations, let's get some things in order to make the transition as smooth and loving as possible.

First, if you have any pending issues with her where you caused hurt in any way that you can recall, you need to ask for forgiveness and address the issues before you can win her heart back. That means you'll have to get a grip on yourself and find a way to bring healing where you caused hurt and that, my friend, will take some effort, wisdom, patience and lots of love. It's a step-by-step process that requires a good support system that is set up to get you the maximum results in regaining your place in her heart. So here are some simple steps to start with:

• FIRST AND MOST IMPORTANT, get help for yourself if you need it, and if your issues are serious, make it professional help.

• LET her know that you realized how bad you screwed up and how you plan to fix the problem. Then talk less of what you're doing and show it with some Love action.

• SHOW her how much you love her by meeting her daily needs which should be priority and primarily emotional. Also ask her if there is something she would like done for her. Just be sensitiveand don't overdo it.

• BE ready to be rejected by her and don't take it personal because she needs to feel secure before she opens up to you.

• DON'T BE afraid to ask her if you could hold her or that you would like to be held.

• TAKE her to some of her favorite places that she enjoys going with you.

• GIVE her as much space and time as she needs to regroup and to think about the relationship.

• KEEP your time with her fresh, creative and exciting.

THIS IS a short list and much more can be added which you can find throughout the book.

If you stay fixated on just loving her, you my friend, will discover a woman who is so beautiful that she'll blow your mind. This will happen because you crawled inside of her mind and made her imaginations run wild.

And woman, if you allow his love to bring healing to your heart and to the relationship, you will discover the real man that you always desired and he will take you to places that will surpass every dream that you ever dreamed.

Gentlemen, you must stay fixated on the outcome because the rewards are amazing and your relationship will be stronger than ever. This whole process will cause you to grow in ways you've never imagined and to find a new love for yourself and for her. The effort must be mutual in maintaining this new level of awareness and love for each other and to live it out whole-heartily.

7

THE OTHER MAN

"BE WISE TO RECEIVE HIM AND BECOME
AWARE AND PREPARE TO DISCOVER YOUR
REAL MAN." —ANTHONY MORALES

*P*reparation helps avoid desperation is a saying that I try to live by daily. This has helped me live a more peaceful life. The life that you're living at the moment is a reflection of the level of preparation that you took when you became aware of a negative situation in your life. It was revealed to you through wisdom, God, the Universe; and if you took action yesterday, today you're enjoying life instead of regretting it. This approach takes confidence and a boldness that activates the courage in you to take the giant and slay him if he so dares to come on your land.

But here's the catch, the giant never comes from the outside; he's lying dormant somewhere in your subconscious mind, your she-motions where you learned certain things throughout your life that have kept you captive in your relationship. There needs to be an evaluation of your perspective of yourself before you can evaluate and prepare yourself to discover your Real Man.

Do you love and know yourself? Or are you so co-dependent on him that if he leaves you, your world will fall apart. Are you still in love with him? Do you believe down deep inside that this relationship will work? Or are you too wounded to keep going? What's really keeping you in the relationship and is it all worth who you really are?

These questions are part of the preparation to discover the real man. Because before you discover the Real Man, you must discover the Real Woman. Let me share some more insight that might be helpful to you. Your man needs your adoration which is vital to him as a man and to the relationship.

Do you know where your man goes for adoration, admiration and appreciation? He goes somewhere. All men do. Does he go to work in hopes of hearing "job well done"? Does he go to the ball field in hopes of hearing "way to go man"? Does he go back home to mother to hear "I'm so proud of you son"? Does he work late in hopes of a few compliments from the women in the office? Does he feast on compliments from patients or clients? Does he hang out at the gym flexing and building his biceps? Tell me, where does your man go to be admired?

* * *

I CAME across this information from the website *Your Tango*, **Kristina Marchant**, which is an example of a tool to use with your man.

* * *

HERE ARE four ways to create a deep bond between you and your man, and
keep him from ever wandering, temporarily or permanently.

OPEN UP **to him**

Your man has to feel comfortable confiding in you. In a world where most men feel they have to act tough just to make it through the day at work or survive a night of beer and football with the guys, they really need a place where they can be vulnerable.

As a woman, you should be the one who creates that vulnerability, inviting space for him. You should create a place for him to take off his "man mask" and just be himself. We all know that men are not like women in the way we talk at length about our problems and speak directly about our feelings, but they do need an outlet for their built-up stress and negative feelings. A woman who can create that outlet is essential to her man's happiness and emotional health. So how do you become a safe place for your man? You make him YOUR safe place first. This includes two steps:

YOU RISK vulnerability with him and share with him your feelings, secrets, fears. Basically, you reveal your underbelly to him.

YOU ALLOW him to comfort you in these moments like he is your hero.

Receiving a man's comfort is important. Surrendering to his hugs, kisses, and soothing words is essential. And even more essential is accepting his comfort graciously and with sensitivity to his ego, even if it doesn't feel comforting. Once you start revealing your underbelly to him and allowing him to comfort you, he will start to open up about his feelings, fears, secrets, needs, and more.

DON'T TALK over him or try to fix his problems by acting like his therapist. Don't half-listen because your sisters on the other line. Be mindful, and in a way that invites him to feel safe and heard in your presence.

* * *

NEVER FIGHT DIRTY.

Now that your man has opened up and shared parts of himself with you, guess what happens with a lot of women? They take these revelations and throw them back in their men's faces in moments of heated argument.

- *"That's why your boss thinks you're weak!"*
- *"No wonder you are afraid of feeling like a failure!"*

• *"Maybe you are acting like that because your father was abusive, like you told me he was."*

When women see red, they want to win a fight and feel like their feelings are valid. But all your feelings are valid. Nothing he says or does is going to negate your feelings. You are entitled to them, and that's all you need to know. If you want your man to hear your feelings, see your hurt, and understand your pain, speak to him like he is someone you hear, see, and understand.

This will create emotional connection and will bring him emotionally close to you. He will realize that you are able to honor his person and his feelings, despite your own negative feelings. He will then start doing the same for you. That's how healthy men work. They want nothing more than to hold your feelings, even when you are upset. They just don't want to get burned for it.

If you can bring your feelings about him to him in a safe environment that invites closeness and positive change, he will break his back trying to honor your feelings and wishes, even if he has to make sacrifices for your happiness. He really wants to take care of your emotional needs.

* * *

SHOW HIM YOU ADORE HIM.

SOME WOMEN ARE NATURALLY open with their physical affection. They touch and caress their man (or everyone they know) lovingly, tenderly, warmly.

These women are goddesses.

It's all about loving touches that soothe the man and invite him into the connection.

Please don't be one of those women whose touches are pulling in nature. Touches that are not caresses, but are more taking in their energy are not mindful touches and push men away.

* * *

Examples:

• *You pull on your husband when you hug him, instead of slowly sinking into deep physical closeness with him.*

   • *You pet your man, but your petting is tense and moves toward you, like you are trying to make him touch you back. (Your petting should move toward his direction.)*

Even more important than touching him is receiving his touch. Anytime your man touches you, relax into it, like he's a hot knife and you're butter on its blade. Melt into his warmth. Let your muscles relax and invite his touch. Sometimes this is easy to do, like during great sex, and sometimes it is hard.

If you are mad at your man, you don't have to force yourself to melt into his touch, but you shouldn't jerk away like he is radiation, either. It feels so horrible to him. If you are mad and hurt, just say that you don't want to be touched; give him a reason why and let him back off. If he doesn't back off immediately, you need to be firm and tell him more forcefully.

* * *

Remember to be playful.

Being genuinely playful requires you to feel happy in your life; therefore, you need to start having a positive, loving relationship with yourself. You should dote on yourself. Take any opportunity to laugh, to have fun, and to relax.

You should make room to feel your negative feelings and be less hard on yourself when you are feeling down. You should take time for you and take care of your mind, body, and soul. You should find a way to love your job and hobbies, and find the joy in them.

Indulge your senses to enhance your sensuality. Once you love yourself in a gentle, playful, forgiving way, and feel inside like you authentically have a positive, playful, feminine, sweet, soft, silly, giggly energy, you can bring that into your relationship.

Take any moment you can to enjoy your man and the moments you share together. Refuse to take anything he does or says too seriously. Find ways to make him warm and smiley and tender and silly inside. I call this "tenderizing him" — you're trying to make his heart tender and juicy, like a filet in the oven.

Happy moments together create emotional intimacy, because laughter makes your hearts happy, and happy hearts are full of love and healing to give to each other.

AFTERWORD

NEVER GIVE-UP

Keep your head up because of who you are. A beautiful, sexy woman; strong, yet gentle; loving, but also firm, intelligent and humble. You're secure about yourself; yet, approachable by others. A man doesn't dictate your life; you've already got that figured out. So, step out into the world and be that woman on fire.

Allow yourself to be free today. Let the world know that you are a woman of respect, dignity and honor, not by what you wear or what you say, but by what's reflected from the inside out. Then stand back and watch what kind of people (men) you will attract.

As a woman, you are precious and valuable. Therefore, you must be very selective of whom you give yourself to (and I don't mean just men) because not everyone will take you to heart and appreciate you.

Today you will have the opportunity to become emotional about something; nevertheless, you must not let it deplete you of who you are, but let it add to your beauty as a woman.

Stop denying yourself those healthy pleasures that make you feel like that special woman that you are. Because at the end of it all, everyone walks away happy and tall and you'll remain empty and lost.

To lower your standards as a woman just to attain a man is a sure sign that you've surrendered your dignity, self-respect and honor. So, before you invest your time (life) in that man, make sure that your return will be greater than your investment, because you are too valuable for a one-night stand.

8

GIVE YOURSELF 100%

#TELLHER PLEDGE

I PLEDGE DAILY TO
        •Invest quality quite time (morning, 15 min.) in myself.
  •Read or listen to self-improvement material — quote, book, audio or video.
  •To love myself unconditionally.
  •Never give up on my dreams.
  •Never give in to discouragement.
  •Accept total responsibility for my life.
  •Take full responsibility for my health.
  •Surround myself with people who love themselves and care about me.
  •Not to live the life of a victim, but to live the life of a victorious woman.
  •To give myself the very best before I give it to other people.

SHARE YOUR PHOTOS and pledges on social media. Be sure to use #tellher so we can find your post and respond personally and or invite you to be a contributor in our next project and or book.

9

FOR HER

FOCUS GROUP FEEDBACK FROM MEN

•$\mathscr{H}$ow does it feel to not be heard?

"WHEN I REALIZE I wasn't heard about something I said before, I feel as if I'm not really her partner and just someone who is there to support her and "release" her tension when needed." —Elvis

•WHEN SHE DOESN'T LISTEN, **how does that make you feel?**

"WHEN SHE DOESN'T LISTEN, I can't explain how it feels. I just go about the rest of my day ready to doing whatever I have to do to keep providing for her and our son." —Billy

•**How do you manage to live through the fact that you can't be free to express yourself with the woman that you love?**

"LIKE MOST GUYS, you just accept it for what it is and you move

on. Sometimes you have other people you share things with."
—Derick

•Why won't you tell how you feel?

"SHE'S SO busy concentrating on what she's going to say next that she hasn't comprehended anything that I've said." —Ivan

•HOW DO YOU FEEL? And what does it do to you when you do share your heart and she is open to hear you out?
"I feel afraid. When she's open, I feel connected and willing to listen to her." —Larry

•WHY DON'T you tell her?
"Just not worth it. As time goes by, I find their ability to hear something about them isn't perfect — it always leads to an argument or them coming back at us with all the flaws in our game." —Miguel

1.WHY DON'T you tell her how you feel?

"I WISH that I could tell her how deep my feelings are for her. I don't tell her because of my fear of being taken advantage of and because previous relationships have not been kind to me."—Mike

1.WHY DON'T you tell her how you feel?

"I DON'T THINK that she really cares what's important to me and if she does, that would have to be explored." —Julius.

1.How do you feel when you share your heart and she is not open?

"When women take interest in their partner's values and goals, he'll know and seek her counsel for support. A lack of comparability can be a real obstacle to deal with. Letting your man know that you support and care about the things that matter to him also goes a long way in the relationship and in communication." —Paul

1.What recommendation to women can help men be more expressive?

I think one of the things women can do to help us men be more expressive with our feelings is to **talk with us** and not question us. Like when on a date, the guy can be genuinely listening by reiterating what she says. We guys like to be listened to as well. —Carl

FOR HIM

FOCUS GROUP FEEDBACK FOR WOMEN

*H*ow important is it that your man expresses himself to you?

"Extremely. Because if he doesn't express his feeling, his heart, and emotions, we will basically have a cold relationship and that's destined to fail." —Pamela

"It is very important as his expression will help me understand him and the situation much better which will give me some clarity."—Daisey

•What are some things that you're doing that stop him from expressing himself?

"Not listening 100% due to past incidents" —Gloria

"Saying things that shut him down." —Mary

•Why can't you control your emotions when he is sharing his heart?

"I usually can control my emotions as I appreciate honesty. If it's a sensitive topic or if it has to do with the way I act or communicate, I get defensive at times". —Nancy

"I'm a bit selfish (I love attention) and I'm too busy trying to explain my emotions" —Bernice

•**Why do women use their partner's past against him in times of arguments?**

"Because it means a woman doesn't fully trust him and down deep inside believes he is not going to change and will repeat his past. —Natasha

"I believe that during our arguments, we feel hurt and can't stick to the topic at the moment."—Carmela

•**What can he do to prepare the moment to share his heart?**

"A sweet call early in the day, and send a card telling her how happy she makes him."—Anita

"He shouldn't start off being aggressive" —Sue

•**"What recommendations do you have for men when expressing their heart?"**

"Express yourself; don't assume a woman doesn't want to hear you out." —Andréa

"Be carefully honest and learn to read her and pay attention". —Karen

11

SELF-DISCOVERY

BEGINS WITH SELF-REFLECTION

*B*y reading and participating in the following reflective exercises, you can improve relationships, including the one you share with God, through a narrative of personal essays.

QUESTIONS FOR **HER** and **HIM** to begin the self-reflecting process and to ignite "Conversations for Self-Discovery."

YOU SHOULD READ through all the questions first so you know what has been or will be asked of your partner in the self-reflecting phase of your journey.

GRAB YOURSELF A JOURNAL, favorite beverage and a writing tablet so you can write freely without and boundaries and only share with your significant other what you wish. You do not have to share anything at all. However, calm and healthy communications is the key!

You can complete this exercise on your own, with your partner or with other couples. I also offer, free complimentary sessions to help you and your partner use these tools. You can schedule a free session on www.thethoughtmaster.com or www.ificouldtellher.com

Remember, you only share what you feel comfortable and any 'Ah-Ha Moments' and I never share and when I do give feedback, I never use anyone's real name.'

ASKING THE RIGHT QUESTIONS IS THE ANSWER

REFLECTION QUESTIONS & EXERCISES

Self-reflection is a necessary step to improving your love life. These questions can be asked regardless of your relationship status. You can be single, married, separated, divorce. Your relationship can be in great standing or very complicated. You can be 21 or 101. There are no right or wrong answers. Answer these questions to get started on the path of self-reflection.

HOW TO COMPLETE THE SELF-REFLECTION EXERCISES:

HOW TO USE THE FOLLOWING SECTION

1. First complete **The Dream Partner Exercise** regardless of your relationship status. We encourage couples to complete it as if they are not in a relationship so they can be honest with themselves and reflect on what they really want in a partner.
2. **Completing the Dream Partner Exercise** will allow you to imagine a perfect spouse. For couples, if you were single again, what would your ideal partner look like. This will encourage you to meditate and will prepare you to answer the following self-reflection questions.
3. Next, complete the **Self-Reflection** questions. You and your partner should write down your answers separately so you can be honest and only if you are comfortable share the answers that you feel that you can laugh and communicate with each other in a positive way.
4. **Schedule your free coaching session** with life enrichment coach **Anthony Morales** to help you and or your partner discuss your results via www.ificouldtellher.com www.thethoughtmaster.com.

MY DREAM PARTNER EXERCISE

EXERCISE FOR ALL (SINGLES, MARRIED, DIVORCE, SEPARATED, IT'S COMPLICATED, ETC.)

*W*hen we are single, we usually have just a vague idea of what our ideal partner might be.

But it is very useful to put time into defining this person, because then when you meet them - you will be able to recognize them straight away!

This tool helps you imagine the qualities of your dream partner.

By asking yourself some questions about your dream partner you can create a clear picture of them in their mind.

When you have finished, you will have a list of the qualities you would like in a future partner.

If you are not single, you will still take the test so you can have a moment to really think about what you want before you begin the reflection process.

Replace "He" and "She" below as appropriate.

QUESTIONS TO DISCOVER YOUR FUTURE PARTNERS QUALITIES

YOU HAVE TO KNOW WHAT YOU WANT IN ORDER TO ATTRACT WHAT YOUR HEART DESIRES

1. What qualities do you want your potential partner to demonstrate?
2. Think about your answers to these questions to get some ideas:
3. "How does he make me feel special?"
4. "What does she do when I'm sick in bed?"
5. "How does he show affection?"
6. "How does he treat me in company when we go out?"
7. "How does he make me laugh?"
8. "Her most important quality is ..."
9. "The best thing about him is ..."

For example:

Question: "How does he treat me in company when we go out?"
Qualities: He is respectful, attentive and kind.

IDENTIFYING YOUR PARTNERS QUALITIES

EXERCISE

*I*n Part I you wrote a list of the qualities of your Future Partner.

But when you meet someone, how will you know if they have those qualities?

Now, write down examples of how they will express those qualities and what actions and behavior will demonstrate those qualities.

For example:

Question: "How does he treat me in company when we go out?"

Qualities: He is respectful, attentive and kind.

Behavior: He is attentive and considerate to me, and kind to the waitress.

YOUR QUALITIES

EXERCISE

*T*his is often the part people overlook.

"Love is not what you get, but what you give."
—Harley M. Storey

1.Now write down the qualities *you* will bring to the relationship.

Part IV: So How Well Do You Know Your Partner?

Do you think you know their favorite movie? What about their favorite day of the week?

This is a fun quiz to do with you and your partner where you're bound to discover a lot of surprises!

1.Get together with your partner.

2.Take one copy each and separately write down the answers you think your partner would give to the following questions.*

3.When you have finished, swap your lists, score each other and laugh!

4.What do you think their...

5.favorite movie is

6.favorite band or singer, or type of music

7.favorite actor, actress

8.favorite season

9.favorite TV show

10.favorite day of the week

11.their hero

12.favorite time of day

13.favorite activity

14.the quality they admire most in others

15.favorite activity

16.best memory together

17.who they are closest to in their family

18.their best friend

19.the personal quality they most appreciate in a partner

20.favorite color

21.their worst habit

22.their best habit

23.kindest thing you have done for them

24.your most difficult habit for them to deal with

25.the hardest issue for them to deal with

26.the one word that best describes them

27.if they were a car what car would they be?

28.what they feel are your three best qualities

29.the thing they would most like you to do

30.what they most want from you

31.the way they would like you to communicate love

32.what is their loving style - how do they demonstrate their love?

*Print two copies of this questionnaire (an easily printable copy on pdf is available in 20 Tools Life Coaches Use® available here) http://www.life-coach-tools.com/free_life_coaching_tools/

18

50 REFLECTION QUESTIONS

EXERCISE

1. What is your maturity level?
2. What is your partner's maturity level?
3. What do you think your partner will say about your maturity level:
4. Do you believe you are acting like a mother or father figure instead of a partner?
5. What is your reaction or response to your partner's immaturity productive or counterproductive? Explain.
6. Do you take time out to love on yourself so that you can meet the challenges of the relationship?
7. How do you and or your partner take time out for yourselves and as a couple? Is it helping? How? Do you to do this more? How will you make this happen?
8. Are you being sensitive to your partner's feelings? (Yes/No) Explain by supporting your answers with examples?
9. Are you ready to hear what's on your partner's mind? Why or why not? Explain.
10. How do you react or respond to your partner in front of the kids and in public when you are upset at him/her? Explain.

11. How does your partner react or respond from your actions above? Explain

12. What can you and or your partner do to improve any negative communications and or yelling that are done in front of children, friends, family and in public?

13. Are you living with a stranger? Have you talked about your childhood with your partner? Do you know your partner's upbringing?

14. Do you believe you know your partner very well? What is stopping you from getting to know your partner's past. What is stopping you from sharing your past with your partner? Explain your answer.

15. How does this answer make you feel?

16. Are you open to hear and feel to what your partner has to say?

17. Are you co-dependent? Is your partner co-dependent? Explain.

18. Do you need your partner to make you happy?

19. Who do you believe in the relationship happiness is prioritized? For example, many men believe their partners should be happy. "Happy Wife, Happy Life." "A diamond is a girl's best friend." Explain, whose happiness come first.

20. Is your partner suppressing his feelings just to keep the peace? Explain.

21. What are you doing about it? Explain.

22. Are you aware of moments when you hurt him? Explain.

23. What do you plan on doing to begin the healing process? Explain.

24. What did you do well today?

25. What your partner didn't do so well today?

26. What would I keep the same about today?

27. What would I change about today?

28. What did I learn about myself by self-reflecting today? (Example: If I had to modify a behavior to help my partner).

29. Do you understand the power that you hold as a woman? And do you know how to use it?
30. Are you aware of your partner's relationship with his mother?
31. How would you explain your partner's rate their relationship?
32. Is manipulation something you use regularly on partner to get your way? Why?
33. Is your main focus on partner's faults or their strengths?
34. Are you happy with yourself? Explain.
35. How do you respond to your partner when they have disappointed you and how does your partner respond to you when you have done something wrong? Explain.
36. Are you or your partner still stuck in a rut?
37. Are you being selfish in the relationship as a woman or man?
38. Do you have a good role model of a man or woman outside of your partner in your life?
39. How has she or he has helped you? How does your partner feel about this person?
40. Are you a Daddy's Girl or Mama's boy?
41. How are you affecting the relationship?
42. Are you living out the role of a man with your woman?
43. Do you understand the role of a male partner and or female partner?
44. Do you know how to confront woman that you love?
45. Are you a woman or man of peace? Explain with examples to support this.
46. Have you sought out the best professional help to improve your role as her man?
47. Are you happy with yourself as a woman or man?
48. Do you take full responsibility for your actions as the man or woman in the relationship? Does your partner support your answer?

49. Are you both giving your best? Are you both giving 100%?
50. How much are you giving her as the man? How much are you giving him as the woman? How can you each give 100% toward the other?

19

WANT MORE?

WE MUST KEEP WORKING ON OUR RELATIONSHIPS. IT'S AN ON-GOING COMMITMENT.

UPDATES, TOOLS, RESOURCES, & STORIES
MS. INDEPENDENT

When I first started coaching Monique in her relationship, she was 29 years old and very independent, smart, and beautiful. She was always surrounded by people of the same lifestyle who were very fond of her and where there was never a lack of men seeking her attention. In fact, Monique came from a family where her parents loved her and where their faith was the main source that kept them together. Then one day she met this young man who caught her attention he was a simple guy that if compared to her previous relationships fell short in many ways; nevertheless, they started dating and within a few months of dating she became pregnant. This obviously was not part of her plan so soon in the relationship, but she accepted the responsibility and a new chapter in her life began. After the child was born, she separated from her partner because of their different lifestyles which were not suitable for the child. This brought on many challenges for a young single mother who came from a family where both parents were in the home and unity was part of their life.

Go online to read more about Ms. Independent and learn how you can share your story with Anthony Morales, and join in on our live conversations and podcasts.

20

EXPLAIN WHY YOUR PARTNER IS A
SHERO/HERO.

YOU CAN USE THIS PAGE TO WRITE OR
DRAW. GRAB EXTRA PAPER AND
HAVE FUN!

HER = Shero!

HIM = Hero!

FOLLOW-UP

TAKE ACTION

Use this space to write any notes or questions you may have and follow up. Anthony needs your feedback for him to continue his journey.

22

RESOURCES

ANYTHING YOU WANT TO SHARE
OR NEED?

Use this space to note any resources or tools you may want to share
or need

23

ONLINE

YOU SHARE YOUR COOL TOOLS WITH
YOUR PARTNER AND OTHERS

Use this space to note any cool websites, tools, or resources you
would like to share to other couples or to your life coach.

24

QUESTIONS

ASK ANTHONY ANYTHING!

Use this space to jot down any questions or concerns you have.

SUBSCRIBE

TO OUR MAILING

WWW.THETHOUGHTMASTER.COM

STAY UPDATED WITH COMPLIMENTARY TOOLS, RESOURCES AND UPDATED VERSIONS OS THIS BOOK BY SUBSCRIBING TO MY MAILING LIST ON **WWW.THETHOUGHTMASTER.COM**

EMAIL: **anthony@thethoughtmaster.com or call 1-84-Thought-1** to help make this book a best seller to reach as many women as possible.

EPILOGUE

"I am constantly trying to communicate something incommunicable,
to explain something inexplicable, to tell about something I only feel
in my bones and which can only be experienced in those bones.
Basically, it is nothing other than this fear we have so often talked
about, but fear spreads to everything, fear of the greatest or of the
smallest, fear, paralyzing fear of pronouncing a word, although this
fear might not only be fear but also a longing for something greater
than all that is fearful."

—Franz Kafka, Letters to Milena

"And a new philosophy emerged called quantum physics, which
suggest that the individual's function is to inform and be informed.
You really exist only when you're in a field sharing and exchanging
information. You create the realities you inhabit."

— Timothy Leary, Chaos & Cyber Culture

"Sometimes, reaching out and taking someone's hand is the beginning
of a journey. At other times, it is allowing another to take yours."

—Vera Nazarian, The Perpetual Calendar of Inspiration

"When you give yourself permission to communicate what matters to you in every situation you will have peace despite rejection or disapproval. Putting a voice to your soul helps you to let go of the negative energy of fear and regret."

—Shannon L. Alder

JAYDEN'S JOURNEY

5 0 1 (C) 3

*J*ayden's Journey is a non-profit founded by Omaida Acevedo for her son, Jayden, who made his transition from his physical body to a new realm. Jayden's Journey continues through him, through us and everyone around us! Omaida's experience and unconditional love for her son has helped her find her purpose which is to serve mothers of children with disabilities and special needs. We need your support to pay the fees associated with becoming a recognizable tax-exempt 501 (c) 3 with the IRS.

You can reach us online to share your story or mail us a letter and donations to:

90 Passaic Street
Garfield, NJ 07026

Please use the donate button to www.thethougtmaster.com or use the contact form to meet to discuss how we can collaborate to serve these beautiful families.

Omaida Acevedo

LET'S COLLABORATE

HERE ARE A FEW SUGGESTIONS

- Featured speaker at upcoming next event(s)
- Guest on my radio show
  www.blogtalkradio.com/thoughtmaster777
- Product Placement on my websites/Guest Blogger
- Networking Events, *"Conversations With Anthony,* "If I Could Tell Her" and *'Couples Hot Spot,* and our charitable events for Jayden's Journey
- Make sure you exchange cards and testimonials and get active with hastags #tellher #anthonymorales, #thethoughtmaster on social media
- Publish Your Story, Photos, Poems and Contributions
- Share your photos and videos using hashtag #TellHer #IFICOULDTELLHER
- Facebook Pages @thethoughtmaster @happyhusbandwifeclub for daily **Live Broadcasts** and our weekly **LIVE podcast** *'The Couples Hot Spot'*
- **www.Instagram.com/thethoughtmaster**
- **www.twitter.com/thoughtmastera**
- **www.facebook.com/thethoughtmaster**

- **www.thethoughtmaster.com www.ificouldtellher.com**
- Internships, Volunteers and Event Planners are invited!

ABOUT THE AUTHOR

ANTHONY MORALES

Like & Follow Anthony Morales On Social Media
Hashtags: #anthonymorales #thethoughtmaster #ificouldtellher
Anthony Morales, a global influencer, motivational speaker, and life
enrichment coach is the author of "If I Could Tell Her' and the creator
of THE THOUGHT MASTER. Visit thethoughtmaster.com for more
Motivational & Inspirational Books & Guides to Goal Setting and
Achieving your Dreams in Life and Business by Anthony Morales
(Life Enrichment Series). Go visit Anthony online
www.thethoughtmaster.com and invite him as a speaker and author at
your next event.

1-84-Thought-1 (1-848-468-4481) (Direct)
anthony@thethoughtmaster.com (Email)

For Bookings, Book Signings and Speaking Engagements
www.thethoughtmaster.com
anthony@thethoughtmaster.com

www.ingramcontent.com/pod-product-compliance
Lightning Source LLC
Chambersburg PA
CBHW070526030426
42337CB00016B/2127